The Hagopian Institute was designed to provide titles of interest to people who want to improve their lives. The series of quote books we have produced are meant to provide inspiration and motivation to people across the world. This particular book is made up completely of quotes from authors long ago. The great minds from B.C. have a lot to offer us in the present time. We believe that you will be surprised by how many of the modern day quotes inspired the very quotes that you use on a daily basis. Some of the greatest minds in the history of the world lived in the years we now know as B.C. We have put together a book with absolutely no fluff. You will find no anonymous quotes, and you will use these references in business speeches, family events, and within your own life to draw inspiration. We have not taken 400 pages to do what around 60 pages could do just as effectively. Please enjoy this book, use the quotes, and let the legends of these great men live on for eternity.

I am indebted to my father for living, but to my teacher for living well

Alexander The Great

I am not afraid of an army of lions led by a sheep; I am afraid of an army of sheep led by

a lion.

Alexander The Great

A tomb now suffices him for whom the whole world was not sufficient.

Alexander The Great

I am dying from the treatment of too many physicians.

Alexander The Great

Remember upon the conduct of each depends the fate of all.

Alexander The Great

There is nothing impossible to him who will try.

Alexander The Great

Everything has a natural explanation. The moon is not a god, but a great rock, and the

sun a hot rock.

Anaxagoras

Men would live exceedingly quiet if these two words, mine and thine, were taken away.

Anaxagoras

As iron is eaten by rust, so are the envious consumed by envy.

Antisthenes

Not to unlearn what you have learned is the most necessary kind of learning.

Antisthenes

Observe your enemies, for they first find out your faults.

Antisthenes

Even when laws have been written down, they ought not always to remain unaltered.

Aristotle

Good habits formed at youth make all the difference.

Aristotle

Education is the best provision for old age.

Aristotle

The roots of education are bitter, but the fruit is sweet.

Aristotle

The one exclusive sign of thorough knowledge is the power of teaching.

Aristotle

Those that know, do. Those that understand, teach.

Aristotle

Bad men are full of repentance.

Aristotle

Change in all things is sweet.

Aristotle

Dignity consists not in possessing honors, but in the consciousness that we deserve them.

Aristotle

Fear is pain arising from the anticipation of evil.

Aristotle

Friendship is a single soul dwelling in two bodies.

Aristotle

Happiness depends upon ourselves.

Aristotle

He who is to be a good ruler must have first been ruled.

Aristotle

It is best to rise from life as from a banquet, neither thirsty nor drunken.

Aristotle

Most people would rather give than get affection.

Aristotle

My best friend is the man who in wishing me well wishes it for my sake.

Aristotle

No excellent soul is exempt from a mixture of madness.

Aristotle

Probable impossibilities are to be preferred to improbable possibilities.

Aristotle

The whole is more than the sum of its parts.

Aristotle

We make war that we may live in peace.

Aristotle

Philosophy is the science which considers truth.

Aristotle

A friend to all is a friend to none.

Aristotle

A great city is not to be confounded with a populous one.

Aristotle

All men by nature desire knowledge.

Aristotle

All paid jobs absorb and degrade the mind.

Aristotle

Character may almost be called the most effective means of persuasion.

Aristotle

Democracy is when the indigent, and not the men of property, are the rulers.

Aristotle

If one way be better than another, that you may be sure is nature's way.

Aristotle

It is the mark of an educated mind to be able to entertain a thought without accepting

it.

Aristotle

Man is by nature a political animal.

Aristotle

Men acquire a particular quality by constantly acting in a particular way.

Aristotle

No one loves the man whom he fears.

Aristotle

Personal beauty is a greater recommendation than any letter of reference.

Aristotle

Pleasure in the job puts perfection in the work.

Aristotle

Quality is not an act, it is a habit.

Aristotle

Republics decline into democracies and democracies degenerate into despotisms.

Aristotle

The law is reason, free from passion.

Aristotle

The most perfect political community is one in which the middle class is in control, and outnumbers both of the other classes.

Aristotle

The secret to humor is surprise.

Aristotle

The worst form of inequality is to try to make unequal things equal.

Aristotle

The young are permanently in a state resembling intoxication.

Aristotle

We are what we repeatedly do. Excellence, then, is not an act, but a habit.

Aristotle

Well begun is half done.

Aristotle

What it lies in our power to do, it lies in our power not to do.

Aristotle

Wit is educated insolence.

Aristotle

No one saves us but ourselves. No one can and no one may. We

ourselves must walk the path.

Buddha

Your work is to discover your work and then with all your heart

to give yourself to it.

Buddha

All that we are is the result of what we have thought. The mind

is everything. What we think we become.

Buddha

He is able who thinks he is able.

Buddha

There are only two mistakes one can make along the road to

truth; not going all the way, and not starting.

Buddha

I found Rome a city of bricks and left it a city of marble.

Augustus

No one is free who does not lord over himself.

Claudius

Better a diamond with a flaw than a pebble without.

Confucius

If a man takes no thought about what is distant, he will find sorrow near at hand.

Confucius

It does not matter how slowly you go so long as you do not stop.

Confucius

You cannot open a book without learning something.

Confucius

What you do not want done to yourself, do not do to others.

Confucius

Choose a job you love, and you will never have to work a day in your life.

Confucius

You cannot open a book without learning something.

Confucius

No matter how busy you may think you are, you must find time for reading, or surrender yourself to

self-chosen ignorance.

Confucius

A superior man is modest in his speech, but exceeds in his actions.

Confucius

Before you embark on a journey of revenge, dig two graves.

Confucius

When you see a man of worth, think of how you may emulate him. When you see one who is unworthy,

examine yourself.

Confucius

Success depends upon previous preparation, and without such preparation there is sure to be failure.

Confucius

Forget injuries, never forget kindnesses.

Confucius

When anger rises, think of the consequences.

Confucius

The man of virtue makes the difficulty to be overcome his first business, and success only a subsequent

consideration.

Confucius

By three methods we may learn wisdom: First, by reflection, which is noblest; Second, by imitation, which is easiest; and third by experience, which is the bitterest.

Confucius

Men's natures are alike, it is their habits that carry them far apart.

Confucius

He who speaks without modesty will find it difficult to make his words good.

Confucius

I hear and I forget. I see and I remember. I do and I understand.

Confucius

Wherever you go, go with all your heart.

Confucius

And remember, no matter where you go, there you are.

Confucius

Do not impose on others what you yourself do not desire.

Confucius

He who learns but does not think, is lost! He who thinks but does not learn is in great danger.

Confucius

I hear and I forget. I see and I remember. I do and I understand.

Confucius

Learning without thought is labor lost; thought without learning is perilous.

Confucius

Life is really simple, but we insist on making it complicated.

Confucius

Never contract friendship with a man that is not better than thyself.

Confucius

Only the wisest and stupidest of men never change.

Confucius

Real knowledge is to know the extent of one's ignorance.

Confucius

The cautious seldom err.

Confucius

The superior man acts before he speaks, and afterwards speaks according to his action.

Confucius

To be wronged is nothing unless you continue to remember it.

Confucius

Virtue is not left to stand alone. He who practices it will have neighbors.

Confucius

We should feel sorrow, but not sink under its oppression.

Confucius

What you do not want done to yourself, do not do to others.

Confucius

When anger rises, think of the consequences.

Confucius

Everything has its beauty but not everyone sees it.

Confucius

He who will not economize will have to agonize.

Confucius

To be able under all circumstances to practice five things constitutes perfect virtue; these five things are gravity, generosity of soul, sincerity, earnestness and kindness.

Confucius

Ability will never catch up with the demand for it.

Confucius

An oppressive government is more to be feared than a tiger.

Confucius

Faced with what is right, to leave it undone shows a lack of courage.

Confucius

Never give a sword to a man who can't dance.

Confucius

To go beyond is as wrong as to fall short.

Confucius

When you are laboring for others let it be with the same zeal as if it were for yourself.

Confucius

By desiring little, a poor man makes himself rich.

Democritus

Good means not merely not to do wrong, but rather not to desire to do wrong.

Democritus

Hope of ill gain is the beginning of loss.

Democritus

It is better to destroy one's own errors than those of others.

Democritus

It is greed to do all the talking but not to want to listen at all.

Democritus

Our sins are more easily remembered than our good deeds.

Democritus

Throw moderation to the winds, and the greatest pleasures bring the greatest pains.

Democritus

I would rather discover a single causal connection than win the throne of Persia.

Democritus

Men should strive to think much and know little.

Democritus

The wrongdoer is more unfortunate than the man wronged.

Democritus

Why not whip the teacher when the pupil misbehaves?

Diogenes of Sinope

There is only a finger's difference between a wise man and a fool.

Diogenes of Sinope

Of what use is a philosopher who doesn't hurt anybody's feelings?

Diogenes of Sinope

The nature of God is a circle of which the center is everywhere and the circumference is nowhere.

Empedocles

Happy is he who has gained the wealth of divine thoughts, wretched is he whose beliefs about the

gods are dark.

Empedocles

A man's character is his fate.

Heraclitus

Justice will overtake fabricators of lies and false witnesses.

Heraclitus

Our envy always lasts longer than the happiness of those we envy.

Heraclitus

The eyes are more exact witnesses than the ears.

Heraclitus

Deliberate violence is more to be quenched than a fire.

Heraclitus

Big results require big ambitions.

Heraclitus

Bigotry is the sacred disease.

Heraclitus

Eyes and ears are poor witnesses to people if they have uncultured souls.

Heraclitus

Hide our ignorance as we will, an evening of wine soon reveals it.

Heraclitus

Much learning does not teach understanding.

Heraclitus

No man ever steps in the same river twice, for it's not the same river and he's

not the same man.

Heraclitus

No one that encounters prosperity does not also encounter danger.

Heraclitus

Nothing endures but change.

Heraclitus

The chain of wedlock is so heavy that it takes two to carry it - and sometimes three.

Heraclitus

The sun is new each day.

Heraclitus

Of all possessions a friend is the most precious.

Herodotus

Civil strife is as much a greater evil than a concerted war effort as war itself is worse than

peace.

Herodotus

All men's gains are the fruit of venturing.

Herodotus

A man calumniated is doubly injured - first by him who utters the calumny, and then by him

who believes it.

Herodotus

As the old saw says well: every end does not appear together with its beginning.

Herodotus

Circumstances rule men and not men circumstances.

Herodotus

Death is a delightful hiding place for weary men.

Herodotus

Great deeds are usually wrought at great risks.

Herodotus

How much better a thing it is to be envied than to be pitied.

Herodotus

Illness strikes men when they are exposed to change.

Herodotus

In soft regions are born soft men.

Herodotus

It is clear that not in one thing alone, but in many ways equality and freedom of speech are a

good thing.

Herodotus

Men trust their ears less than their eyes.

Herodotus

The destiny of man is in his own soul.

Herodotus

The most hateful human misfortune is for a wise man to have no influence.

Herodotus

Experience is the teacher of all things.

Julius Caesar

I came, I saw, I conquered.

Julius Caesar

As a rule, men worry more about what they can't see than about what they can.

Julius Caesar

Cowards die many times before their actual deaths.

Julius Caesar

I love the name of honor, more than I fear death.

Julius Caesar

Fortune, which has a great deal of power in other matters but especially in war, can bring about great changes in a situation through very slight forces.

Julius Caesar

In war, events of importance are the result of trivial causes.

Julius Caesar

It is not these well-fed long-haired men that I fear, but the pale and the hungry-looking.

Julius Caesar

Which death is preferably to every other? "The unexpected".

Julius Caesar

I have lived long enough both in years and in accomplishments.

Julius Caesar

If you must break the law, do it to seize power: in all other cases observe it.

Julius Caesar

It is better to create than to learn! Creating is the essence of life.

Julius Caesar

It is easier to find men who will volunteer to die, than to find those who are willing to

endure pain with patience.

Julius Caesar

Men are nearly always willing to believe what they wish.

Julius Caesar

No one is so brave that he is not disturbed by something unexpected.

Julius Caesar

When I let go of what I am, I become what I might be.

Lao Tzu

Violence, even well intentioned, always rebounds upon oneself.

Lao Tzu

To the mind that is still, the whole universe surrenders.

Lao Tzu

To see things in the seed, that is genius.

Lao Tzu

The power of intuitive understanding will protect you from harm until the end of your

days.

Lao Tzu

The journey of a thousand miles begins with one step.

Lao Tzu

Respond intelligently even to unintelligent treatment.

Lao Tzu

Mastering others is strength. Mastering yourself is true power.

Lao Tzu

An ant on the move does more than a dozing ox.

Lao Tzu

When the best leader's work is done the people say, "We did it ourselves."

Lao Tzu

To lead people walk behind them.

Lao Tzu

Those who have knowledge, don't predict. Those who predict, don't have knowledge.

Lao Tzu

The softest things in the world overcome the hardest things in the world.

Lao Tzu

The people are hungry: It is because those in authority eat up too much in taxes

Lao Tzu

Silence is a source of great strength.

Lao Tzu

One who is too insistent on his own views, finds few to agree with him.

Lao Tzu

Nature does not hurry, yet everything is accomplished.

Lao Tzu

Knowing others is wisdom, knowing yourself is Enlightenment.

Lao Tzu

If you do not change direction, you may end up where you are heading.

Lao Tzu

He who talks more is sooner exhausted.

Lao Tzu

Great acts are made up of small deeds.

Lao Tzu

Govern a great nation as you would cook a small fish. Do not overdo it.

Lao Tzu

Give a man a fish and you feed him for a day. Teach him how to fish and you feed him

for a lifetime.

Lao Tzu

Born to be wild - live to outgrow it.

Lao Tzu

Anticipate the difficult by managing the easy.

Lao Tzu

Friends are the siblings God never gave us.

Mencius

Great is the man who has not lost his childlike heart.

Mencius

Knowledge is true opinion.

Plato

The direction in which education starts a man will determine his future.

Plato

You are young, my son, and, as the years go by, time will change and even reverse

many of your present opinions. Refrain therefore awhile from setting

yourself up as a judge of the highest matters

Plato

People are like dirt. They can either nourish you and help you grow as a person or

they can stunt your growth and make you wilt and die.

Plato

If a man neglects education, he walks lame to the end of his life.

Plato

The direction in which education starts a man will determine his future in life.

Plato

The beginning is the most important part of the work.

Plato

Hardly any human being is capable of pursuing two professions or two arts rightly

Plato

We are twice armed if we fight with faith.

Plato

A good decision is based on knowledge and not on numbers.

Plato

All the gold which is under or upon the earth is not enough to give in exchange for

virtue.

Plato

Any man may easily do harm, but not every man can do good to another.

Plato

Be kind, for everyone you meet is fighting a hard battle.

Plato

Better a little which is well done, than a great deal imperfectly.

Plato

Death is not the worst that can happen to men.

Plato

For a man to conquer himself is the first and noblest of all victories.

Plato

Good actions give strength to ourselves and inspire good actions in others.

Plato

I shall assume that your silence gives consent.

Plato

It is right to give every man his due.

Plato

Justice means minding one's own business and not meddling with other men's

concerns.

Plato

Knowledge becomes evil if the aim be not virtuous.

Plato

Let parents bequeath to their children not riches, but the spirit of reverence.

Plato

Life must be lived as play.

Plato

No law or ordinance is mightier than understanding.

Plato

Nothing in the affairs of men is worthy of great anxiety.

Plato

There is no harm in repeating a good thing.

Plato

Only the dead have seen the end of the war.

Plato

Be kind, for everyone you meet is fighting a hard battle.

Plato

Wise men talk because they have something to say; fools, because they have to say

something.

Plato

We can easily forgive a child who is afraid of the dark; the real tragedy of life is

when men are afraid of the light.

Plato

A hero is born among a hundred, a wise man is found among a thousand, but an

accomplished one might not be found even among a hundred thousand men.

Plato

Apply yourself both now and in the next life. Without effort, you cannot be prosperous.

Though the land be good, You cannot have an abundant crop

without cultivation.

Plato

The learning and knowledge that we have, is, at the most, but little compared with

that of which we are ignorant.

Plato

There are two things a person should never be angry at, what they can help, and what

they cannot.

Plato

Ignorance, the root and the stem of every evil.

Plato

When men speak ill of thee, live so as nobody may believe them.

Plato

Courage is knowing what not to fear.

Plato

Friends have all things in common.

Plato

Courage is a kind of salvation.

Plato

Opinion is the medium between knowledge and ignorance.

Plato

At the touch of love everyone becomes a poet.

Plato

The greatest wealth is to live content with little.

Plato

Thinking: the talking of the soul with itself.

Plato

Nothing in the affairs of men is worthy of great anxiety.

Plato

Life must be lived as play.

Plato

Good actions give strength to ourselves and inspire good actions in others.

Plato

As the builders say, the larger stones do not lie well without the lesser.

Plato

Astronomy compels the soul to look upwards and leads us from this world to another.

Plato

Attention to health is life greatest hindrance.

Plato

Cunning... is but the low mimic of wisdom.

Plato

Democracy passes into despotism.

Plato

For good nurture and education implant good constitutions.

Plato

He was a wise man who invented beer.

Plato

He who steals a little steals with the same wish as he who steals much, but with less

power.

Plato

Honesty is for the most part less profitable than dishonesty.

Plato

I have hardly ever known a mathematician who was capable of reasoning.

Plato

Knowledge which is acquired under compulsion has no hold on the mind.

Plato

Love is a serious mental disease.

Plato

No evil can happen to a good man, either in life or after death.

Plato

No one ever teaches well who wants to teach, or governs well who wants to govern.

Plato

Opinion is the medium between knowledge and ignorance.

Plato

Philosophy begins in wonder.

Plato

Rhetoric is the art of ruling the minds of men.

Plato

The excessive increase of anything often causes a reaction in the opposite direction.

Plato

The heaviest penalty for deciding to engage in politics is to be ruled by someone inferior to yourself.

Plato

The measure of a man is what he does with power.

Plato

The wisest have the most authority.

Plato

There are three classes of men; lovers of wisdom, lovers of honor, and lovers of gain.

Plato

They do certainly give very strange, and newfangled, names to diseases.

Plato

Those who are too smart to engage in politics are punished by being governed by those who are dumber.

Plato

Wealth is well known to be a great comforter.

Plato

When there is an income tax, the just man will pay more and the unjust less on the same amount of income.

Plato

A few vices are sufficient to darken many virtues.

Plutarch

Those who know how to win are much more numerous than those who know how to make proper use of their victories.

Polybius

There are two sides to every question.

Protagoras

Man is the measure of all things, of things that are that they are, and of things that are not that they are not.

Protagoras

During war, the laws are silent.

Quintus Tullius Cicero

Avoid any specific discussion of public policy at public meetings.

Quintus Tullius Cicero

Necessity makes even the timid brave.

Sallust

A good man would prefer to be defeated than to defeat injustice by evil means.

Sallust

All who consult on doubtful matters, should be void of hatred, friendship,

anger, and pity.

Sallust

Do as much as possible, and talk of yourself as little as possible

Sallust

Think like a man of action, and act like a man of thought.

Sallust

Ambition breaks the ties of blood, and forgets the obligations of gratitude.

Sallust

Ambition drove many men to become false; to have one thought locked in the breast, another ready on the tongue.

Sallust

As the blessings of health and fortune have a beginning, so they must also find an end. Everything rises but to fall, and increases but to decay.

Sallust

Every bad precedent originated as a justifiable measure.

Sallust

Every man is the architect of his own fortune.

Sallust

Everything that rises sets, and everything that grows, grows old.

Sallust

Harmony makes small things grow, lack of it makes great things decay.

Sallust

He that will be angry for anything will be angry for nothing.

Sallust

In my opinion it is less shameful for a king to be overcome by force of arms than by bribery.

Sallust

It is better to use fair means and fail, than foul and conquer.

Sallust

Just to stir things up seemed a great reward in itself.

Sallust

No man underestimates the wrongs he suffers; many take them more seriously than is right.

Sallust

The glory that goes with wealth is fleeting and fragile; virtue is a possession glorious and eternal.

Sallust

We employ the mind to rule, the body to serve.

Sallust

It is the part of a fool to say, I should not have thought.

Scipio Africanus

I'm never less at leisure than when at leisure, or less alone than when alone.

Scipio Africanus

Though bitter, good medicine cures illness. Though it may hurt, loyal criticism will have beneficial effects.

Sima Qian

Wisdom begins in wonder.

Socrates

The unexamined life is not worth living.

Socrates

The greatest way to live with honor in this world is to be what we pretend

to be.

Socrates

It is not living that matters, but living rightly.

Socrates

Beware the barrenness of a busy life.

Socrates

Worthless people live only to eat and drink; people of worth eat and drink

only to live.

Socrates

We are what we repeatedly do. Excellence, then, is a habit.

Socrates

My advice to you is get married: if you find a good wife you'll be happy; if

not, you'll become a philosopher.

Socrates

If a man is proud of his wealth, he should not be praised until it is known

how he employs it.

Socrates

I was really too honest a man to be a politician and live.

Socrates

From the deepest desires often come the deadliest hate.

Socrates

As to marriage or celibacy, let a man take which course he will, he will be

sure to repent.

Socrates

The general who wins the battle makes many calculations in his temple

before the battle is fought. The general who loses makes but few

calculations beforehand.

Sun Tzu

Opportunities multiply as they are seized.

Sun Tzu

You have to believe in yourself.

Sun Tzu

Can you imagine what I would do if I could do all I can?

Sun Tzu

When envoys are sent with compliments in their mouths, it is a sign that

the enemy wishes for a truce.

Sun Tzu

Victorious warriors win first and then go to war, while defeated

warriors go to war first and then seek to win.

Sun Tzu

Thus, what is of supreme importance in war is to attack the enemy's

strategy.

Sun Tzu

There is no instance of a nation benefitting from prolonged warfare.

Sun Tzu

The supreme art of war is to subdue the enemy without fighting.

Sun Tzu

Strategy without tactics is the slowest route to victory.

Tactics without strategy is the noise before defeat.

Sun Tzu

Secret operations are essential in war; upon them the army relies to make

its every move.

Sun Tzu

Pretend inferiority and encourage his arrogance.

Sun Tzu

Know thy self, know thy enemy. A thousand battles, a thousand victories.

Sun Tzu

Invincibility lies in the defense; the possibility of victory in the attack.

Sun Tzu

If you are far from the enemy, make him believe you are near.

Sun Tzu

He who knows when he can fight and when he cannot, will be victorious.

Sun Tzu

He who is prudent and lies in wait for an enemy who is not, will be

victorious.

Sun Tzu

All warfare is based on deception.

Sun Tzu

The skilful employer of men will employ the wise man, the brave man, the

covetous man, and the stupid man.

Sun Tzu

Time is the most valuable thing a man can spend.

Theophrastus

History is Philosophy teaching by examples.

Thucydides

Ignorance is bold and knowledge reserved.

Thucydides

We secure our friends not by accepting favors but by doing them.

Thucydides

Be convinced that to be happy means to be free and that to be free

means to be brave. Therefore do not take lightly the perils of war.

Thucydides

An avowal of poverty is no disgrace to any man; to make no effort to

escape it is indeed disgraceful.

Thucydides

Few things are brought to a successful issue by impetuous desire, but

most by calm and prudent forethought.

Thucydides

It is frequently a misfortune to have very brilliant men in charge of

affairs. They expect too much of ordinary men.

Thucydides

Men naturally despise those who court them, but respect those who do

not give way to them.

Thucydides

The secret of freedom, courage.

Thucydides

I have often repented speaking, but never of holding my tongue.

Xenocrates

It takes a wise man to recognize a wise man.

Xenophanes

The sweetest of all sounds is praise.

Xenophon

Fast is fine, but accuracy is everything.

Xenophon

Those whose character is mean and vicious will rouse others to

animosity against them.

Xun Zi

The person attempting to travel two roads at once will get

nowhere.

Xun Zi

Pride and excess bring disaster for man.

Xun Zi

I once tried thinking for an entire day, but I found it less valuable

than one moment of study.

Xun Zi

The rigid cause themselves to be broken; the pliable cause

themselves to be bound.

Xun Zi

CPSIA information can be obtained at www.ICGtesting.com
Printed in the USA
LVOW09s1448030816

498911LV00005B/223/P

9 781434 895554